IT'S COOL TO LEARN ABOUT COUNTRIES

Social Studies Explorer

PAKISTAN

➻ by Ellen Labrecque

CHERRY LAKE PUBLISHING • ANN ARBOR, MICHIGAN

NOV 1 9 2010

CHERRY LAKE Publishing

Published in the United States of America
by Cherry Lake Publishing
Ann Arbor, Michigan
www.cherrylakepublishing.com

Content Adviser: Tithi Bhattacharya, PhD, Associate Professor of History,
Purdue University, West Lafayette, Indiana

Book design: The Design Lab

Photo credits: Cover and page 1, ©Mudassar Ahmed Dar/Shutterstock, Inc.; cover
(stamp), ©iStockphoto.com/acprints; page 4, ©Pichugin Dmitry/Shutterstock, Inc.;
page 7, ©iStockphoto.com/gniedzieska; page 8, ©Fabienne Fossez/Alamy; pages 10,
13, 14, 15, 16 and 25, ©ASSOCIATED PRESS; page 11, ©Drimi/Dreamstime.com; page
12, ©Naiyyer/Shutterstock, Inc.; pages 17, 18 and 24, ©iStockphoto.com/danishkhan;
page 20, ©Tom Allwood/Alamy; pages 21, 22 and 29, ©iStockphoto.com/Mr_Khan;
page 23, ©Grafoo/Dreamstime.com; page 27, ©Lorraine Chittock/PhotoLibrary;
page 28, ©iStockphoto.com/luxG4; page 30, ©Picture Contact/Alamy; page 31,
©Shariffc/Dreamstime.com; page 32, ©Associated Sports Photography/Alamy; page
34, ©Shadow69/Dreamstime.com; page 36, ©Louise Batalla Duran/Alamy; page
37, ©iStockphoto.com/PaulCowan; page 38, ©iStockphoto.com/JoeGough; page 39,
©iStockphoto.com/VikramRaghuvanshi; page 44, ©iStockphoto.com/thinqkreations;
page 45, ©Eva Gruendemann/Shutterstock, Inc.

Library of Congress Cataloging-in-Publication Data
Labrecque, Ellen.
  It's cool to learn about countries: Pakistan/by Ellen Labrecque.
      p. cm.—(Social studies explorer)
  Includes index.
  ISBN-13: 978-1-60279-828-1 (lib. bdg.)
  ISBN-10: 1-60279-828-1 (lib. bdg.)
  1. Pakistan—Juvenile literature. I. Title. II. Title: Pakistan. III. Series.
  DS376.9.L325 2011
  954.91—dc22
                                          2009049105

Cherry Lake Publishing would like to acknowledge the work of The Partnership for
21st Century Skills. Please visit www.21stcenturyskills.org for more information.

Printed in the United States of America
Corporate Graphics Inc.
July 2010
CLFA07

TABLE OF CONTENTS

CHAPTER ONE

WELCOME TO PAKISTAN

➻ Pakistan offers a mix of ancient and modern sights.

Pakistan is in the news a lot. Many times, it is for negative events that occur there, such as political unrest. At its core, however, Pakistan is a beautiful land with wonderful people. This is the Pakistan to get to know and love.

The Islamic Republic of Pakistan is the nation's official name. It is located in South Asia. This long, narrow country is approximately twice the size of California.

It spans 307,374 square miles (796,095 square kilometers). Pakistan has more than 167 million residents. Pakistan also boasts many different landscapes. The North is a mountain climber's paradise. The South features tropical beaches along the Arabian Sea. Deserts and plains are found between the two extremes.

Pakistan is bordered by Afghanistan and Iran to the west. China is to the north, and India is to the east. The Arabian Sea runs along the southern border. The country is divided into four areas, or **provinces**: Sindh, Punjab, North-West Frontier Province, and Balochistan. Each province has its own capital.

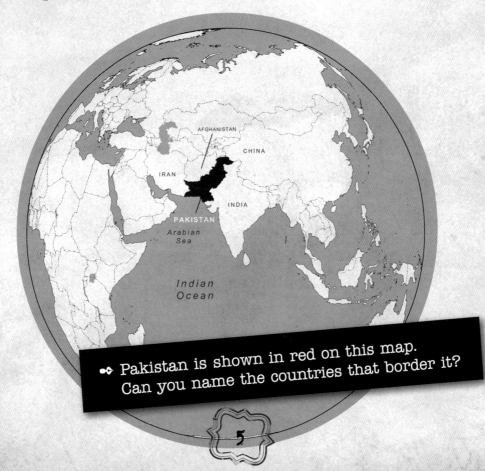

Pakistan is shown in red on this map. Can you name the countries that border it?

Sindh is located in the southern part of Pakistan. It is home to the country's largest city and main seaport, Karachi. Karachi is also Sindh's capital. It is Pakistan's center of banking and industry.

Punjab is in the eastern part of the country. It is Pakistan's most populated area. Why? The Indus River flows through there. The river and its streams help make this region Pakistan's most fertile farming area. Lahore is Punjab's capital. The country's capital, Islamabad, is also in Punjab.

The Indus River is approximately 1,800 miles (2,900 kilometers) long. People depend on the Indus River as their main water source.

● Ascending K2 is dangerous for even the most experienced mountain climbers.

The North-West Frontier is the northernmost province of Pakistan. This is the country's most mountainous area. K2, the world's second highest peak, is located here. It is 28,251 feet (8,611 meters) above sea level. Near Peshawar, the region's capital, is a passageway called the Khyber Pass. It is a major route between Afghanistan and Pakistan.

To the west and south of the North-West Frontier, is an area of Pakistan called the Federally Administered Tribal Areas (FATA). There are seven main tribal areas in FATA. Officially, the Pakistani president governs the area. But tribal elders, called *maliks*, are in charge of day-to-day activity.

Balochistan is on Pakistan's southwestern border alongside Iran. The capital is Quetta. This region is the least populated area of Pakistan. Most of the land is dry.

◆ These children live in a small village in Balochistan.

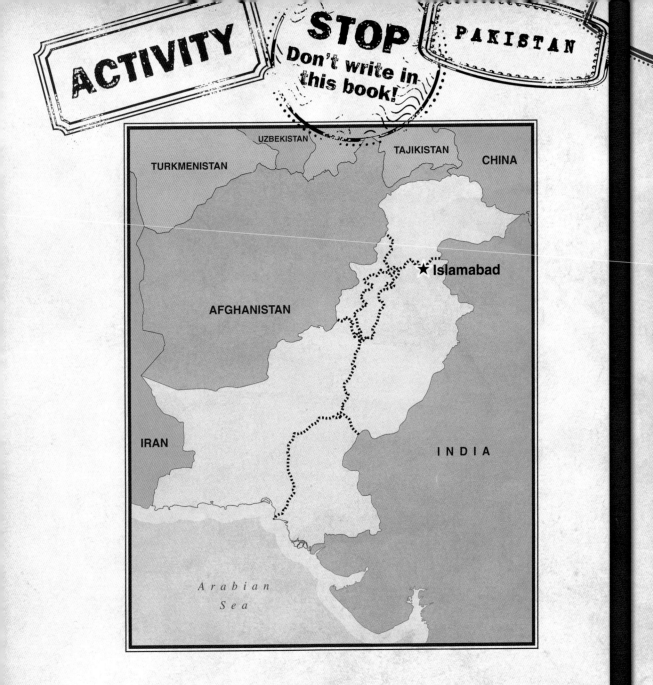

Look at the map of Pakistan and its surrounding neighbors. Using a separate sheet of paper, trace Pakistan. Follow the dotted lines that divide Pakistan into each of the provinces and FATA. Using the information in this chapter, label each area.

Pakistan's climate varies greatly, from frozen mountaintops to hot beaches. Most of Pakistan, however, has three different seasons. The hot season begins in March and runs through June. The wet season lasts from July through September. The cold season runs from October through February. During the hot season, temperatures in some places can reach 122 degrees Fahrenheit (50 degrees Celsius)! In certain areas during the cold season, the temperature can drop well below freezing.

➡ Roads, fields, and homes are sometimes flooded during the wet season.

❦ The markhor is an endangered species.

The wet season in Pakistan is not that wet. Only about a quarter of the country gets more than 10 inches (25.4 centimeters) of rain each year.

Pakistan is filled with amazing animals and plants. The country's national animal is the flare-horned markhor. The markhor is a wild goat with horns that curve in spirals. They are found in the mountain regions. Snow leopards also live in the mountains. They are one of Pakistan's most **endangered** animals.

CHAPTER TWO

BUSINESS AND GOVERNMENT IN PAKISTAN

The Minar-e-Pakistan was built in honor of the country's independence.

The country of Pakistan had a difficult birth. Before declaring independence in 1947, Pakistan, along with present-day India and Bangladesh, was part of British India. That year, the region was split into two separate, independent countries: Pakistan (East and West), and India.

This partition, or division, was made according to religion. Pakistan was intended for the Muslim population. India was intended for the Hindu population. In the first years of independence, some 7.2 million Muslims fled to East and West Pakistan. The two parts of the country were separated by India. Likewise, approximately 10 million Hindus who had been living in Pakistan fled to India. Millions who moved were driven by force. It was hoped that the partition would keep the peace. At first, it did the opposite. Muslims living in India and Hindus in Pakistan were threatened, beaten, or killed to drive the minority populations out. Nearly one million people died.

➜ Muslim passengers fill a train in India, waiting to leave for Pakistan in 1947.

Many more people died in the following decades as Pakistan continued to redefine its borders. A civil war broke out in 1971 between East and West Pakistan. The East declared itself independent from the West. India sided with East Pakistan. The combined military force defeated West Pakistan in less than 2 weeks. Today, East Pakistan is known as the country of Bangladesh.

Mohammed Ali Jinnah was Pakistan's first president. Jinnah is considered Pakistan's founding father and held the title of Quaid-e-Azam, or "Great Leader." Jinnah worked hard to encourage peace during the fighting that followed independence.

Mohammed Ali Jinnah

● A woman casts her vote in Rawalpindi in 2008.

Pakistan's government has had an interesting history. Today, Pakistan follows a federal **parliamentary** system. The president is the head of state. The prime minister is the head of government. In the election of 2008, the people elected the president. The prime minister was elected by the National Assembly. The responsibilities of each position have changed through the years. The president holds the power and can dismiss the prime minister at any time.

For a large part of Pakistan's history, the government has been led by the military. There have been four military takeovers since Pakistan declared independence in 1947. Each time the military took over, the government system was dissolved.

Since 2002, an elected official has run Pakistan. Asif Ali Zardari was elected president in 2008. Yousuf Raza Gilani became his prime minister. The president is elected to a 5-year term and can only be reelected once. The president also selects the governor of each of the four provinces.

Benazir Bhutto was voted prime minister of Pakistan in 1988, and again in 1993. She was the first woman to be an elected leader of a Muslim country. In December 2007, Bhutto was assassinated along with three other political candidates. The assassinations took place during a spike in political violence in the country.

Benazir Bhutto

↝ Some neighborhoods in Pakistan are overcrowded, with little access to good housing or clean water.

Since its formation, Pakistan has struggled to build up its economy. Pakistan is a country filled with very rich and very poor people. Half of the country's wealth is held by only 20 percent of households. As much as one quarter of the population lives in poverty. Many more struggle not far above that level. Poverty involves much more than not having enough money. It involves a person's ability to access what he or she needs to live. This includes food and safe drinking water, shelter, and medicine. It also includes access to opportunities such as education.

Most of the nation's poor live in **rural** Pakistan. They farm and raise livestock. Because Pakistan has so little rain, most farmers do not depend on rainfall. Instead, Pakistan has one of the largest **irrigation** systems in the world. Canals bring water from the Indus River to farm fields. Wheat, rice, and sugarcane are the country's leading crops.

❖ Agriculture is a big part of life for many Pakistanis.

Two-thirds of Pakistan's people make their living by farming and raising livestock. Farming, however, only provides 22 percent of the country's income. The country's biggest business is in textiles. Textile mills make cloth from cotton, silk, and jute. Pakistan's **exports** are mainly cotton textiles and manufactured clothes. Factories also produce leather goods such as shoes, boots, and coats.

IMPORT EXPORT

Do you want to know more about Pakistan's economy? Then take a look at its trading partners. Trading partners are the countries that **import** goods from a country or export goods to that country. Here is a graph showing the countries that are Pakistan's top import and export trading partners.

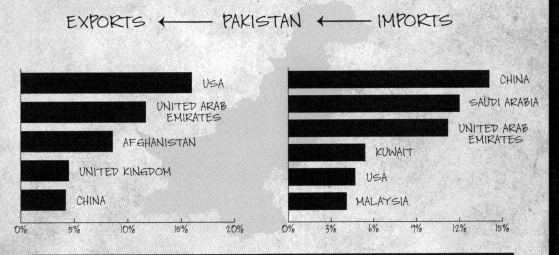

EXPORTS ← PAKISTAN ← IMPORTS

EXPORTS:
- USA
- UNITED ARAB EMIRATES
- AFGHANISTAN
- UNITED KINGDOM
- CHINA

(0%, 5%, 10%, 15%, 20%)

IMPORTS:
- CHINA
- SAUDI ARABIA
- UNITED ARAB EMIRATES
- KUWAIT
- USA
- MALAYSIA

(0%, 3%, 6%, 9%, 12%, 15%)

These factories affect the poor living in the country. More than 3 million children work in the textile factories. They often work long, unpaid hours—sometimes only in exchange for food and shelter. They often miss out on school and recreation. With help from the United Nations and other international organizations, the Pakistani government has worked to improve these issues. Since 2001, the percentage of people living in poverty has dropped by approximately 10 percent. Improvement is slow, but the work continues.

➼ A young boy works in a shawl factory in Pakistan.

STOP
Don't write in this book!

RUPEES

Pakistan's basic unit of money is the rupee. It is made up of 100 paisas. In 2010, one U.S. dollar equaled approximately 84.4 rupees. Using a calculator, convert the following U.S. dollar amounts into rupees on a separate sheet of paper. See below for the answers.

    a.) $5.00 = _____ rupees
    b.) $10.00 = _____ rupees
    c.) $20.00 = _____ rupees

Answers: a.) $5 \times 84.4 = 422.0$ rupees; b.) $10 \times 84.4 = 844.0$ rupees; c.) $20 \times 84.4 = 1,688.0$ rupees

CHAPTER THREE

MEET THE PEOPLE

❧ Pakistani culture includes a variety of languages, ethnicities, and religious beliefs.

Pakistan was founded as an Islamic country. In Pakistan, 95 percent of the people are Muslim, or followers of Islam. The Qur'an is a book of religious teachings. It is central to their religion.

There are five especially important duties of the Islamic faith known as the Five Pillars. The first is to make a formal statement of belief in Islam. The second requirement is to pray five times each day. The third pillar is to give donations of food and money to the poor. The fourth is to fast during the holy month of Ramadan. The final pillar requires those physically and financially able to make a journey to Mecca at least once.

Many Muslims go to a **mosque** for their daily prayers. They line up in rows behind an imam, who leads them in prayer. The Shah Faisal Mosque is Pakistan's largest. The main prayer hall and courtyard can hold 100,000 people!

Shah Faisal Mosque

There are five major ethnic or cultural groups in Pakistan. They are Punjabi, Sindhi, Pashtun, Balochi, and Muhajir. Most of the groups can be associated with specific provinces.

Approximately half of Pakistanis are Punjabi. Many Punjabis work as farmers in the Punjab's Indus Valley. Many government officials and members of the army are also Punjabis. Sindhis mainly live in the rural areas of Sindh. Pashtuns work as herders, farmers, and traders. They live mostly in the North-West

Three Sindhi women take a break from farm work.

➥ Balochi herders sometimes move between Afghanistan and Pakistan.

Frontier Province and FATA. Balochis in Balochistan are **nomadic**. They move their sheep and goats across the dry Baluchistan **plateau**. Muhajirs are the **refugees** who fled to Pakistan during the partition in 1947 and 1948. Most settled in cities.

There are also several thousand Afghan refugees in Pakistan. Refugees began leaving Afghanistan in 1979, fleeing Soviet military action. Since then, they have continued to enter Pakistan because of civil war and, most recently, U.S. military actions.

The national language of Pakistan is Urdu. Business is often done in English. More than 20 other languages are spoken in Pakistan. Most are tied to a region or ethnicity, such as Punjabi.

Through its history, Urdu has traded words and phrases with other languages spoken around it. These have included Persian, Arabic, Hindi, and English. The Urdu words below have either been influenced by the English language or adopted into English in some form. Can you guess what each word means? See below for the answers.

1. plet _____
2. machiz _____
3. pyjama _____
4. dactr _____

Answers: 1-plate; 2-matches; 3-pajamas; 4-doctor

❧ Most marriages in Pakistan are arranged
by the families of the bride and groom.

Families are a central part of daily life. Tradition plays a large part in how a family is run. Men are considered heads of the family. Women run the household and raise the children. Several generations of a family live together under the same roof.

Marriages are usually arranged by a couple's parents. The bride is usually younger than the groom, often in her late teens. A **dowry** is included in most arranged marriages. The parents of the bride give her money and things such as jewelry to bring to her new husband.

Some families in Pakistan are more traditional than others. Many observe a tradition called purdah. Purdah is the Muslim practice of preventing women from being seen by men. Women are separated in the household by walls, screens, or curtains. When a woman goes outside, she wears a burqa. A burqa cloaks her entire body, including her face.

➳ A burqa might be blue, black, or cream colored.

● Some women might wear hijab, using scarves to cover their heads.

Other women dress in pants and show their faces in public. Many of them live in the cities, where they attend school or work. Some live in the country, where they work on farmland. Work in farm fields makes the practice of purdah difficult.

Only 60 percent of the population attends school. Many children have to work to help support their families. Also, many families don't believe in educating women. Approximately half of the population is literate, or can read and write. Most illiterate people live in the rural areas where access to school is limited.

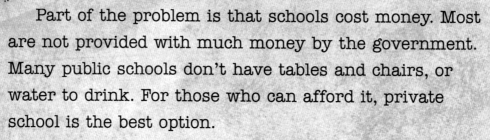

Part of the problem is that schools cost money. Most are not provided with much money by the government. Many public schools don't have tables and chairs, or water to drink. For those who can afford it, private school is the best option.

Through the last few years, more private schools have been built in Pakistan. In fact, roughly 11 million of the country's 33 million students now attend private schools.

❖ Some schools are funded by the United Nations or other organizations.

CHAPTER FOUR

CELEBRATIONS

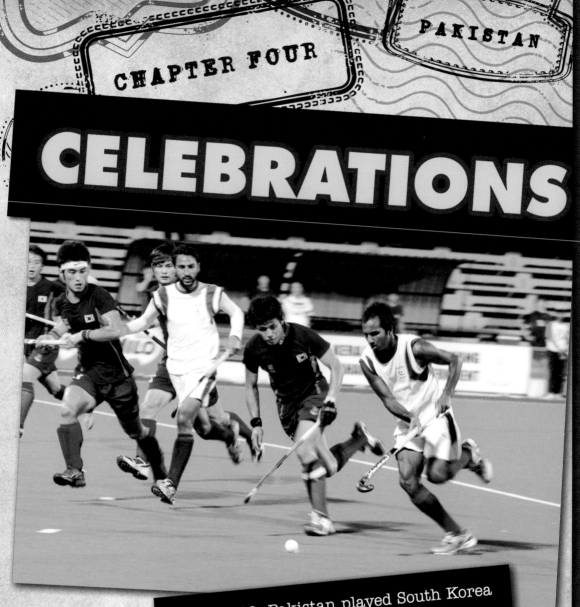

↝ In 2009, Pakistan played South Korea in the Asia Cup Hockey Final.

Pakistanis have a variety of ways to have fun. Athletics are very popular. Field hockey is the country's national sport. One of the most popular sports is cricket. Cricket is similar to baseball in that it is played with a ball and bat.

Some of the world's best cricket players, such as Imran Khan and Asif Iqbal, have come from Pakistan. In 1992, Pakistan won the cricket World Cup. This event is considered the most important cricket competition in the world.

Poetry is an important part of Pakistan's culture. People go to poetry readings, called *mushairas*. Typical poems are about romantic love and love for God. In recent years, more poems have addressed politics. The hardships of Pakistan's poor is another common subject.

Many times, poems are set to music. *Qawwali* is a type of song that uses lyrics from religious poetry. *Ghazals*, or short romantic poems, are also often set to music. Listening to Pakistani radio, you might hear classical music pieces, called *ragas*. You might also hear modern pop music. But some of the most popular tunes on the radio are *filmi* songs. As you might guess from the name, this music comes from popular movies made in Pakistan or neighboring India.

Pakistan has a huge pop music scene. The music is popular around the world. "Dil Dil Pakistan" by the Pakistani rock band Vital Signs was voted the third most popular song in the world in a BBC poll. These days, people listen to bands such as Jal and solo singers, such as Ali Zafar.

PAKISTAN পাকিস্তান
40 PAISA
POSTAGE
WARSAK PROJECT
1958 1960

♡ Dil Dil Pakistan

One place to hear wonderful music is at a wedding ceremony. At a traditional Pakistani wedding, the ceremony is conducted outside under a large tent. The bride and groom say special prayers and perform wedding rituals. The *quazi*, or religious leader, performs the ceremony. Afterwards, guests eat, sing, and dance.

Pakistani music fans attend concerts such as this one featuring Ali Zafar (far left).

Before a Pakistani wedding, the bride's hands and feet are painted in decorative patterns with henna paste. Henna paste is a reddish dye. Below are two designs. On a separate sheet of paper, try drawing the designs yourself. The patterns are detailed. Using a thin colored pencil for your sketches works best.

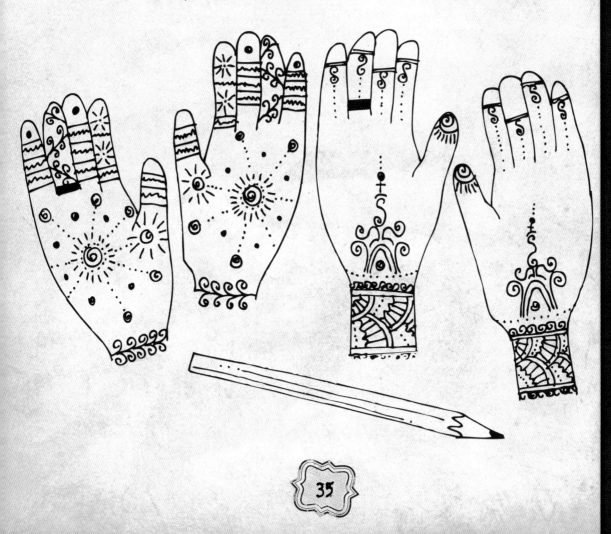

Islam has two major celebrations, or *eids*, during the year. One is called Eid al-Fitr. It marks the end of Ramadan. Ramadan is the month of fasting, in which people don't eat or drink each day from dawn until sunset. The act of fasting is said to redirect the heart away from worldly activities and cleanse the soul. It also allows Muslims to practice self-discipline, sacrifice, and sympathy for those who are less fortunate. Each year, Eid al-Fitr falls after 29 or 30 days of fasting.

On the first morning of the celebration, everybody goes for special prayers. They are held in open fields or

◆ *Eid Mubarak means Happy Eid!*

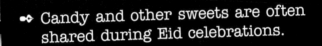

•◦ Candy and other sweets are often shared during Eid celebrations.

mosques. Children receive gifts and money. Many times, the streets have fairs with music, dancing, and games.

The other major celebration is called Eid al-Adha. This celebration is based on the story of the prophet Abraham. He was willing to sacrifice his son, Ishmael, to God to prove his love. When God saw that Abraham was willing to sacrifice Ishmael, he stopped him and had him kill a lamb instead. During Eid al-Adha, an animal is slaughtered in remembrance. One third of the meat is given to the poor, one third to friends, and the rest is shared by the family. There is also gift giving and a lot of eating during this celebration.

CHAPTER FIVE

WHAT'S FOR DINNER?

↦ Some dishes are made with vegetables. Others have meat, rice, or both.

The people of Pakistan enjoy plenty of mouthwatering foods. Most people eat three meals each day. Breakfast is the lightest meal. Dinner features many dishes served all at one time. People tend to eat dinner as late as 9 p.m. When visitors stop by at mealtime, they are always invited to share the food with their hosts.

Most Pakistanis eat with their hands. They always use the right hand. The left hand is reserved for tasks such as taking off shoes. Most of the diet is made up of rice, vegetables, and meat. Pakistanis also eat a traditional bread called *roti*. Muslim Pakistanis never eat pork because it is considered unclean.

❧ Roti is often served warm with meals.

Mithi roti is a type of sweet flatbread. You can eat it for breakfast or as a snack. This recipe requires using a stovetop and working with hot oil. Be sure to have an adult help. Here's what you'll need:

Mithi Roti

INGREDIENTS

2 cups (256 grams) whole wheat flour, plus more for kneading and rolling (you could also use chapati flour)

1 tablespoon (6.2 grams) brown sugar

warm water

2 to 3 tablespoons (29.6 to 44.4 milliliters) vegetable oil

INSTRUCTIONS:

1. Combine the flour and water into a bowl. Start with 2/3 cup (158.5 ml) of water. Add slightly more water if the dough is too dry. Add more flour if the dough is too sticky.

2. Knead well until you have a tender mass of dough. Let it sit for approximately 15 minutes.

3. Take a glob of dough that is slightly larger than a golf ball. Work it into a ball.

4. Flour the rolling pin and your work surface. Using the pin, roll the dough into a flat circle.

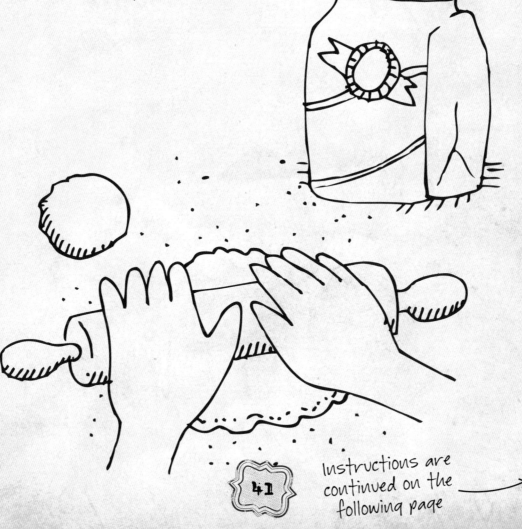

Instructions are continued on the following page →

5. Use a pastry brush to evenly spread a layer of oil over the surface of the dough.

6. Start at one edge of the dough. Using your fingers, roll up the dough from one edge all the way to the opposite edge. You should have what looks like a snake. Next, work this tube of dough into a coil, almost like a cinnamon bun.

7. Use your palm to press the dough flat. Roll it out with the rolling pin.

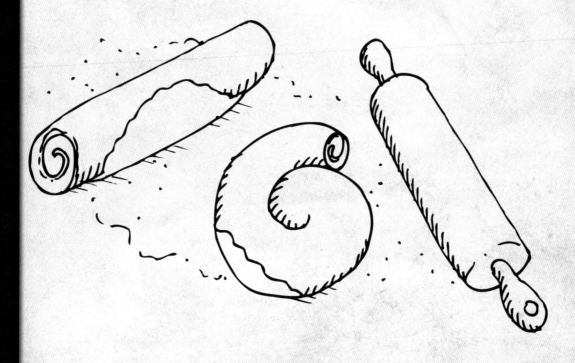

8. Have an adult heat 1 tablespoon (14.8 ml) of oil in a pan.

9. Once the oil is warm, carefully lay the roti dough in the pan.

10. After 1 minute, add another layer of oil and a sprinkling of brown sugar on top of the roti. Spread evenly with the pastry brush. Use a spatula to carefully flip the roti over.

11. The bread is finished when both sides are golden brown.

12. Repeat Step #3 through Step #10 until you've used all the dough.

Enjoy!

The Pakistani menu offers plenty of yummy sweet treats as well. Jalebis are one example. They consist of a deep-fried batter dunked in sticky sugar syrup. Pakistan's version of ice cream, called *kulfi*, is also a favorite.

Pakistanis also drink tea. People show their hospitality by offering tea to guests.

A lot of Pakistani dishes are seasoned with masala. Masalas are special blends of spices. Families often have their own favorite masala recipe.

PAKISTAN

40 POSTAGE PAISA   WARSAK PROJECT   1955 1960

❧ Masala recipes can change according to the chef or the dish being made.

Mango is a popular flavor of lassi.

Another popular drink is *lassi*. It is a yogurt-based drink that many people enjoy on hot days. Many people add their own favorite ingredients. Some include honey, cinnamon, mint, mango, and banana.

This nation of millions has faced many obstacles throughout its history. It will likely face many more. Have you enjoyed your tour of Pakistan?

dowry (DOU-ree) the valuables that women of certain cultures bring with them when they marry

endangered (en-DAYN-jurd) at risk of dying out completely

exports (EK-sportss) act of selling something to another country or products sold in this way

import (IM-port) bring in from another country

irrigation (ihr-uh-GAY-shuhn) the supplying of crops with water by manmade means, such as pipes

mosque (MAHSK) a Muslim place of worship

nomadic (noh-MAD-ik) having to do with groups that wander from place to place, with no fixed home

parliamentary (par-luh-MEN-tur-ee) having to do with the group that has been elected to make the laws in certain countries

plateau (pla-TOH) an area of high, flat land

provinces (PROV-uhnss-iz) regions of certain countries

refugees (REF-yuh-jeez) people who are forced to flee their homes

rural (RUR-uhl) having to do with the country or farming

FOR MORE INFORMATION

Books

Crompton, Samuel Willard. *Pakistan*. New York: Chelsea House Publishers, 2007.

Donaldson, Madeline. *Pakistan*. Minneapolis: Lerner Publications Company, 2009.

Wachtel, Alan. *Pakistan*. Vero Beach, FL: Rourke Publishing, 2009.

Web Sites

Central Intelligence Agency—The World Factbook: Pakistan
www.cia.gov/library/publications/the-world-factbook/geos/pk.html
Check out this site for information about Pakistan's economy, geography, population, and government.

National Geographic—Pakistan Facts
travel.nationalgeographic.com/travel/countries/pakistan-facts/
Find a general overview of Pakistan at this helpful resource.

TIME for Kids—Pakistan
www.timeforkids.com/TFK/kids/hh/goplaces/main/0,28375,1612047,00.html
Explore information about Pakistan's history and more at this informative site.

INDEX

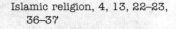

ABOUT THE AUTHOR
Ellen Labrecque has written many books for young readers. She loves traveling—especially to other countries. She and her husband, Jeff (also a writer), and their two children live in New Jersey.